PROFESSION & ECONOMY FROM THE TRUE HUMAN PERSPECTIVE

EROL ERBAS
-HUMAN-

No part of this publication may be reproduced, distributed, or transmitted in any form or by any means, including photocopying, recording, or other electronic or mechanical methods, or by any information storage and retrieval system without the prior written permission of the publisher, except in the case of very brief quotations embodied in critical reviews and certain other noncommercial uses permitted by copyright law.

Copyright © 2022 Cozum Kendimiz

All rights reserved.

www.cozumkendimiz.com

ISBN: 9798835053810

PREFACE

There are a few foundations upon which we build our lives. The economy and our professional lives are two of the foundations on which we stand. They allow us to show our humanity, to socialize, and to demonstrate our character. Since ancient civilizations, these two issues have played a significant role in social life. They contributed to the climate of peace, trust, and respect by developing and progressing naturally, with no bad consequences.

The drifting away from human nature in professions and the economy over the ages, has been one of the main reasons putting pressure on society and causing social unrest, particularly in the last one hundred years.

The shift in priority from human to material things, as well as the dominance of material goals, are not accepted by society's conscience because they go against human nature. Since there has been no science for true human needs until now, we have become entangled in an inextricable web of problems.

For those of us looking for an answer to these problems, Erol Erbas has made presentations in light of the practices he has positively confirmed in his life.

Mr. Erbas has discussed his professional and economic experiences throughout his career as an educator, as well as a variety of other topics related to human beings.

The discourses on profession and economy in this book are taken from Mr. Erbas's spontaneous answers to questions posed during his lectures, influenced by his life experience, without any contribution to his words.

♦

"These books are to be enriched and updated as the human renews, produces, expands, and improves by each moment and the lives of humans in the future will become richer. Words get renewed and gain meaning according to lives lived."

Erol Erbas
Human

Website
www.erolerbas.com

CONTENTS

CHAPTER 1 1

PROFESSION 1

   WE NEED TO BE PRODUCERS 3

   THOSE WHO ARE DRIVEN BY WEALTH CANNOT HAVE A PROFESSION 4

   CRAFTSMAN, TRADESMAN, MERCHANT 6

   NO IDEA ABOUT THE TRUE HUMAN NATURE 8

LEARNING OF PROFESSION 10

   GAINING EXPERIENCE 11

   BEING SKILLED AND QUALIFIED 12

   LEADERS OF PROFESSIONS LEAD THE WAY 14

   ENCOURAGING INNOVATION 15

   TECHNOLOGY PROGRESSES ACCORDING TO DEMAND 15

LABOR 17

   EFFICIENCY AT WORK 18

   HOBBY 19

   PLANNING AND DREAMS 20

PRINCIPLES OF DOING BUSINESS 22

   GETTING RESULTS 23

Governance	*24*
We must have enough knowledge for ourselves	*25*
Deception	*26*
Increasing efficiency	*28*
Benefiting or harming people	**30**
A true human enhances	*32*
Work ethic	**34**
Being fair	*35*
Chapter 2	**37**
Economy	**37**
The system was established by exploiters	*39*
Moving from the broken economic system	*40*
Employee - employer	*41*
Taxation	*42*
Capital	**43**
There is no place for humanity when capital enters	*44*
The middlemen	**46**
Who is responsible for this overpricing?	*47*
Money	**49**
Money is a value measurement	*50*

EARNING MONEY AND SUCCESS **51**
    LIFE IS ABOUT TRUST *52*

WEALTH..**54**
    CREATING AND DISTRIBUTING WEALTH................................. *55*
    YOU ARE WEALTHY BY NATURE *56*
    FIVE IDOLS.. *57*

SHOPPING **60**
    NOT KNOWING THE PROFESSION OF SHOPPING *61*
    THE ISSUE IS TO BUY FOR ITS TRUE VALUE................................ *62*

WASTEFULNESS - FRUGALITY **64**
    THE ONE WHO WASTES BECOMES NEEDY *65*
    EXPENSE – WASTE *66*

GIVING PRIORITY TO PEOPLE..**67**
    VALUING PEOPLE *68*

Why don't we humans research ourselves when we are researching everything else?

THE WANDERER
(Dreamer, Daydreamer)

THE ONE WHO BREATHES
(The Spirit, Core, Sustainer of Life)

THE BODY
(The Created, Home, Servant)

- - → Conscience
- - → The Home of the One Who Breathes (Gönül)

" Read - Educate   Live - Inspire "

The key to power is to lean on The One Who Breathes.

MORALITY is being consistently efficient.

EROL ERBAŞ
- HUMAN -

THE HUMAN; is the one who takes ownership of the moment.

FOR HUMANITY;

the age of interpretation,
likening, fabricating,
daydreaming, narratives,
imitating and vanity has ended.

NOW...

**The age of living in the moment
attention, authenticity, efficiency,
success, trust, respect, love,
and ownership** has begun.

NOTHING is more valuable
than my integrity.

IF I DO IT, IT WILL HAPPEN.

EROL ERBAŞ
- HUMAN -

"

You cannot speak about anyone, but yourself.
You cannot speak to anyone, but yourself.
You cannot know anyone, but yourself.
If you don't know your self, you know nothing else.

CHAPTER 1

PROFESSION

People have two parts, there is the economic part, and then there is the internal part. (*explained in the book "Ourselves") The internal part produces, the external part consumes. It is necessary to provide for the needs of the external part. How can this be achieved? With nature. Air, fire, water, earth are the four main elements. With those elements, the needs of the external body are met. In order to provide, we do research and development, and work in a particular profession for ourselves. In the past, there were professions such as coachmen and coppersmiths. There were tinsmiths, there were blacksmiths, there were cutlers... Today, as we provide to fulfill our needs, our professions have different names. With these professions, our identity will be remembered.

To begin with, everyone should have a profession. A profession is what you produce but producing alone is not enough; you should also advance in your expertise. How can we have satisfaction without producing? If there were true professionals today, they wouldn't make us wear these synthetic fabrics. Synthetic fabric is not good for us. Do manufacturers think about that? They don't. They think about exploiting. They think about reducing production costs at the expense of quality or well-being.

Why are you in your profession? To be able to feed yourself? To make a living? To make some money? If these are the reasons you are in your profession, then you will not find peace. When a person is working just to make a living, to earn some money, just for the sake of working or to kill some time; there is no higher purpose in these aims. It's not necessary to show your personality when you are driven by these goals. So, what should we do? We should say: "I will become successful."

We need to be properly equipped to support ourselves economically and also to be independent. We need to have a profession. Some people may be owners of a factory, but they do not own their profession. A series of events leads them to become rich but similarly, a single event may cause bankruptcy. But for those owning a profession, this is not the case. Even if they fail, they go and start a new business, and they keep running it to success.

We Need To Be Producers

The economic system was built on production. When a person does not produce and is not successful in their profession, they cannot become a true human. A person needs to have a profession, even more so, they need to be a producer. So, if I am a producer and if I am successful in my profession, I will not have financial difficulties.

We should work hard; we should produce a lot. But we are wasting a lot of time. Today's system is created so that people have time to kill. Television programming is created in this way, social life is designed in this way, work-life is designed in this way; it's the same everywhere. For example, municipalities are always building parks for people. Why are they building parks? For people to come and relax. That's good but why not build laboratories or workshops? Open a laboratory, let people come, develop themselves in whatever field, and come up with inventions.

Everyone should innovate in their profession. It is just not OK if you don't innovate at all in your work.

There has to be some innovation. What innovations can you come up with? For example, for months I have not used any negative words. See, this is innovation. We need to make an effort and innovate.

I wonder about something. I have never seen anyone who would speak about their profession, except for a few people. I mean, if you are a teacher you would talk about teaching, wouldn't you? If you are an industrialist, you would talk about the industry. If you are a doctor, you would talk about medicine. If you are an engineer you would talk about engineering. But I have never seen it. There is always a discussion about other issues. There is a lot of advising others, a lot of talk about other people's failures or shortcomings. No one would ever see me talking outside of my profession. This is how I understand that I have a profession, "Character and Personality Education". One who has a profession talks about their profession.

THOSE WHO ARE DRIVEN BY WEALTH CANNOT HAVE A PROFESSION

Nowadays we have the wrong understanding of "profession". Whenever we hear about the opportunity to earn easy and free money, we go after it. We don't pay attention to our own profession. Instead, just because there was some person, who got rich in some way, we think we can also be rich in the same way. When you disregard your character and integrity, and only care about money and how to become rich, then you will think about deceiving and exploiting someone. If you want to become rich with this mentality, without a doubt, you will overpower and oppress others.

Everyone should have only one profession. What is the reason for having more than one? Maybe you just heard about an opportunity, and you started a job unnecessarily. You said to yourself, "This is a good business, I will do it too". For example, the government provides funding for livestock farming and suddenly the "white collars" enter that market. A job they never saw or knew anything about. It makes me laugh. They can only suffer huge losses and fail to profit. Their only concern is some free funds for a few years. This is not right. You should leave your mark with what you do. Like in the past, there were ropemakers, tinsmiths, coppersmiths. They would work to leave their marks. No one has this intention anymore. We are living in vain when we live like this. You do not take care of your spouse or your family as much as you busy yourself with problems at work. You have gotten used to it this way and you just keep it going. That won't work. We need to readjust. A person should have one job and they should devote the rest of their time to humanly purposes. Then we would have happiness and joy in our lives.

For a person, one home and one business are enough. You should also have a profession. That is it. I need "me" for myself. If you establish two businesses, you cannot master a profession. You become a middleman. If you establish three businesses, you really become a middleman. But there is no place for middlemen in the true-human perspective. Everyone should master their professions, and become producers. This is fundamental. This should be the system for finding true happiness.

Craftsman, Tradesman, Merchant

The most valued people in the world are craftsmen. What is their core value? Craftsmen have the vision to provide something that's the best, most beautiful, most pleasant; something that will bring comfort to people. This is their main concern, not the profit.

There is a certain standard for being a craftsman. When one can renew oneself, he or she is a craftsman. If one can renew oneself in a month, a week, a day; he or she is a craftsman. Craftsmen must present their crafts. Craftsmen are practitioners. They produce, present and practice but innovation is always a must.

The tradesman promotes the craftsman's innovation and advertises it. Tradesmanship means gaining the trust of people. In other words, customers must trust a tradesman. For example, if you are selling curtains, but not producing them, you are not owning the profession. You are simply a tradesman for curtains. You should exude trustworthiness to people. This is tradesmanship. Do we have such trust in trade today? Unfortunately, not. Everyone shops with the fear in the back of their mind of being cheated. This is not what tradesmanship is.

Merchants are very powerful. Wherever they are; they bring honor and dignity to their professions, as well as basic human needs such as food, drink, clothing, shelter. Everything is asked from the merchants. But merchants today are merely exploiting. See, these are only merchants in body, not in spirit. Always evaluate things from two sides; first, outer appearance, and second, true human nature. The merchant by true human nature will present the best quality, efficiency, and beauty. Trading doesn't mean exploitation.

To be a merchant means to be accountable, that they will provide for the needs of their region in their particular field. There is no consideration of money here. Money is the last thing on their mind. It is only a reward for their success. It will come naturally. There is no place for humanity when your main goal is just to earn money.

No idea about the true human nature

I am saying this very clearly; there is no doctrine or common teaching about the character and personality aspects of the true human nature. Rather, the common knowledge is mainly based on the physical aspect of human beings. I call this; work - earn - eat - drink - sleep. Animals in the barn do this as well. But I am a human. I should be different. There is no doctrine about the true human nature. Because there is no doctrine like this, we are dealing with various exploitations. Those who exploit create widespread fear by saying, "the population is increasing, there will be a famine!" Good grief! Tomorrow there could be some great invention, like a small pill that will satisfy your hunger. Those concerns are groundless.

If everyone would train just one person in their profession, would anyone be left unemployed? By doing this, you would have paid the dues of your profession. Instead of empowering people to become self-sufficient in a profession, we are using the economic system of the exploiters which makes hungry people even hungrier. The exploiters established an economic system that promotes poverty. When you "aid" those in poverty, you make them dependent on you, which keeps them in poverty. Why is there hunger today? Because of the impoverished not taking enough initiative. You won't take action if you think "some way or the other, the help will come". It is the same way everywhere. People will not take action when they think that help will come anyway. In the villages where I grew up, it would be considered shameful to receive aid. It hurts your self-respect. And yet, today we are proud of providing this kind of aid, where we give as opposed to empowering.

LEARNING OF PROFESSION

Everyone has their own unique talent and we should all choose a profession based on this. For example, if this city needs ten thousand bakers, there would be that many people who have baking as their primary skill. If five thousand butchers are needed, that many people would have butchery skills. There is a need for ten thousand tailors, one thousand engineers... Skills are developed according to the needs of that society. This is how nature works. But if the one with engineering talent becomes a baker, and the one with a baking talent becomes an engineer, that's where the problem starts. Would a person thrive in a profession they do not like? If you don't love your profession, you won't be truly successful. A person should do what they love, according to their abilities and their nature.

We prepared an activity for children ages four to six. We provided them with various toys used in different professions. For a day or two, children were drawn to the toys that they saw at home or on television. Then they gravitated to their natural profession, which was related to their abilities and talents. There was a parent who wanted her son to become a doctor. During the activity, her son showed interest in cooking. She said, "I will make him a doctor". But this child loved cooking.

A person's natural profession is best identified when they are a child. Later on, children should work in their natural profession and go to school at the same time. Once they become an adult, they will have a full-fledged profession and will be able to manage their budget. What happens to children if you don't give them any guidance or raise them without fostering their natural skills?

GAINING EXPERIENCE

Why don't you encourage your sons and daughters to work or get a summer job? Children aged 10 to 15 are in their aspirational period. They have various ambitions, they aspire to many different things some of which may even be concerning to parents, which may cause trouble. Some parents may be pleased to say, "My child is doing well in school and behaving well". But if we took those kids out of the classroom and placed them in an environment where they had to face hardship, how many of them would be able to stand on their own? Children need to develop certain skills outside of the classroom to flourish later in life. We should raise our children to be well-rounded.

I am delighted when I see a new business struggle. Why? Because when they struggle, they gain experience. If someone inexperienced gets their hands on a well-established business, they will ruin it, they will get into all sorts of trouble. But if they struggle in the early stages of their business, they will be able to see the full picture, to understand the value and the significance of how it grew to become a successful one. Each time we overcome an obstacle; we grow. If we avoid them, we stay small. The one with strong character will go and overcome the obstacles.

BEING SKILLED AND QUALIFIED

To ensure a good standard of living, we study and get a degree. Is this enough to be a well-rounded person? Why are jobs not simply given to anyone coming out of a university? Because of lack of skills and qualifications. Why are we not skilled and qualified enough? For one thing, many were raised in their childhoods to be lazy in two ways. First, you were constantly told that you were too little to do whatever you wanted to do, and second, you were dismissed whenever you tried to help. For example, what do we hear on television when children start a school vacation? "Give your children a break". Who says that? Experts. Do they really know best? How can they give that advice? We, on the other hand, make sure that our children start chores when they are two or three years old.

Older people would probably know more about this. Think about old villages; people knew how to mow with a scythe, knew how to care for farm animals, knew how to maintain a farm, knew how to bury their dead, knew how to maintain relationships with their neighbors, knew how to grow wheat and make bread. This is how they gained skills to survive. However, these qualifications nowadays are missing at universities. The average university student does not know the basics of shopping nor manages to maintain a balanced budget. They don't know how to bargain. They are grown-ups but most of them are still financially dependent on their parents. This is not right. This is not what education should be about. Education should lead us to bring out the skills and talents we have and make a person more capable of facing the hardships in life.

Today skilled labor is divided into different branches. Forestry, agriculture, textile, metallurgy, ... There are so many different fields. Why is that? Because of diversification. As a result of this, a person, for example, knows how to build a wall but does not know how to apply plaster; knows how to hammer wood, but does not know how to lay iron rods. Why is that? If you go to some small towns in Anatolia, men there do every type of work. These new trends haven't gotten there yet. They cannot make glass, but apart from that, they can make all parts of a new house; the same person makes the doors and the windows among other things. When professions are divided into so many branches, we are left unskilled and unqualified.

Leaders of Professions Lead the Way

If you are one of the notable people in a certain profession and in a position to educate, you need to stay ahead or else, the students may surpass you. Then, you're no longer a leader of that profession. This is critical. You will remain the leader if you maintain the lead in the competition. An example of a leader in their profession is Mimar Sinan, an architect. Why is he an example? Because his best works are the ones at the end of his career. He always nourished and improved his apprentices. If he had stayed on the level of his earlier works, the others in his profession would have taken the lead.

ENCOURAGING INNOVATION

There should be a laboratory for a profession in every home. For example, a dentist should have a dental laboratory, a teacher should have a teaching laboratory. When possible, they can do research and analysis in that laboratory. They can come up with inventions using their intelligence and labor, and for a hundred years, the inventor should have rights to that invention.

If you have an invention, you should receive the rights for the innovation for the time of its validity. Regardless of where in the world this innovation is used, 10% of the profit should be yours. Thus, we pave the way for competition, success, innovation, and invention. In today's world, someone comes up with an innovation and some big company snatches it right away, they use it themselves and capitalize on that inventor's idea.

TECHNOLOGY PROGRESSES ACCORDING TO DEMAND

I value two expressions: "I can do it" and "We'll make it happen". There are no limits to what people can do. If there is something that is not yet solved, that does not mean it is unsolvable; it means, it will be solved in the future. Let me say something even more thought-provoking; technology progresses with the growth in the human population. New technology is developed as a law of nature, depending on the increase in population. If a cell phone is needed, the idea strikes someone. And then he can say: "I invented it". We think that "we" did something but how could we think it if the idea didn't come to our minds? God works his acts through his people. These innovative ideas come to humans' minds from our innate divine nature. In recent decades the population has grown largely, so there will be more and more innovations. The speed of new inventions is determined by the population.

LABOR

When a person is engaged in truly fulfilling work, getting tired wouldn't cross his mind. He would feel pleasure from working. The work is not fruitful where there are workers who think about tiredness. Tiredness would be an indicator that work for them is just a means to an end. People who wait just to clock out cannot find happiness. Those who are constantly pursuing success are happy.

Hardworking is actually in our true nature, but we were not taught well enough. Starting when we were just a baby, they gave us a pacifier, they made us accustomed to the softer beds, they rocked us to sleep, they got us used to just sitting and listening. How many families are making their child do the chores with them? We let them sleep, eat, drink, but hey, "do not get involved, do not do the work, do not go to the kitchen; I had to do those as a child, so, I will spare you..." How many families have shared with their child the pleasure of working or grabbed them by the hand and taught them to work? The lack of all this, leads to some children becoming rebellious in their teenage years and we are unable to deal with them.

Efficiency at Work

In the mornings when we wake up, instead of getting right out of bed most people just stay there tossing and turning. Do you immediately jump out of bed right after you wake up? That's the way to become fully awake and ready for the day. Getting out of bed immediately after opening your eyes helps us to be more productive throughout the day. I am ready to make a bet; if one jumps out of bed early in the morning and works hard, they will finish all their work before noon. Then afterward enough time will remain to innovate, develop, invent, and produce in their field.

Do people really go and work hard for eight hours straight? No. Their mind is somewhere else; thinking about cars, thinking about friends, thinking about neighbors, thinking about the coming games. They sit at their desk and wait for time to pass. This is not the way to work. I am sure that in general, most people are not mentally present at work for more than half an hour a day. Their body is there but where is their mind? Who are they angry with? From whom are they expecting something? By whom are they annoyed?

The life of an inactive, idle man is toxic. Do you want me to prove it? Just look at one of your free days. You waste your time worrying about things that did not happen, you are annoyed by your family members... This is an invention of those who want to exploit people; on Sundays, everyone is sitting idle at home. Just think about what kind of thoughts come to you when you're inactive. Like a mirror, I am showing you to yourself. An idle person's life is toxic. This is very normal; what would an idle man do? The ones who exploit said; do nothing productive on Saturdays and Sundays, and just consume. Just see how much squandering this is. Just think. What if we were productive on the weekends? How much improvement would there be? Productivity is not only about work, it can be in any field, at any place.

Hobby

I have hobbies in my spare time. If I have free time, I search for water. I go to the mountains and drill for it. I stop when I see some greenery in the mountains (as a sign of water), I find an excavator nearby and get them to dig. That excavator hits the ground, and then it hits again. Water starts dripping like from the tip of a needle. "He is always searching for treasure", they often say about me. True, I am searching for gold, but my gold is blue. Not yellow. The water will serve for thousands of years. It would be nice if, as a result of my work, someone could wash their face when passing by. You will be able to feel that happiness when someone feels good doing that. Other than that, I plant a lot of trees. I plant flowers. I clean the district. I also do soil conservation. These are my hobbies. A hobby is a particular activity apart from your profession, that is good for society. I don't consider it a hobby if it is just a time-wasting activity.

PLANNING AND DREAMS

We should plan the things that we want to do. Planning means thinking out what you are going to do. For example, when I go to search for water, I first try to locate the area where water can be found. Then, we get prepared with the excavator. In the morning; we leave, we take the excavator, we search for water. We wait for two days after we find water, just to be sure that the water flow will not cease. I do further planning while I wait. I systematize the pipe types, the wrench, the ropes, and the top nylon. I prepare whatever I need without missing anything. Why? I should be able to finish in one day what may take one week for others to do. This is only possible with planning. We get in the car, go and we return after finishing work the same day. Otherwise, instead of one day it would take eight days: "let us do this tomorrow, let us do that tomorrow..." Planning is for making our job faster, to accelerate and to systematize.

We are confusing dreams with plans. Plans are my command; they are my work with a project and an outline. The dreams are something that I am not working toward, hoping from someone else. There are no calculations for dreams. Plans are what I have to fulfill; in dreams, there are only expectations and hopes. For example, a student wants to become a doctor. What he needs to do is set a goal, make a plan, and study. But instead, he dreams. He did not even take the exam yet, but in his dreams, he already examines patients, performs surgeries, and acts like a hero. Similar to this, you visualize the things you want, and you make them come true only in your dreams. Remember this; nothing happens the same way as it happens in your dreams.

PRINCIPLES OF DOING BUSINESS

We cannot do everything on our own, but we need to have some knowledge about the things we do. For example, we go to buy a car and we ask the salesperson about the dimensions, and we get a, "this is not my field, ask the other guy, he knows" answer. We ask about the engine, and we get an "ask him over there, he knows". We ask about the steering, and we get an "ask that one over there, she knows". For information about one car, they send us to three different people and still, that business makes a profit. Profiting in this way is just wrong; how is it possible? If I were working there for five minutes, I would know everything. I would learn all about those cars if I were standing there all day.

If I am going to spend eight hours a day in a company as an employee, I would impress the employer with my skills so that they would never want to let me go. The only reason they would terminate my employment would be if they thought I was corrupt and of no use to them or doing harm in some way. Simple as that. It amazes me how an employee would go to their superiors to ask simple questions such as the dimensions or the weight of a product they are selling. These are the first things that come to mind for me, how is it possible that the responsible salesperson would not know the answers to these questions. They should easily be able to inform the customer about things like, what substance it is made from, the weight, the ingredients; so on and so forth. The first time I visit the seller I ask about everything. I am an observer. This is the reason why phony professionals and people with so-called degrees avoid me as a customer.

GETTING RESULTS

We need to get results in what we do. The other day while I was looking out the window, an old man and his daughter came to this student dormitory across the street, they tried to get in but the doors were locked. They both tried to open the doors but couldn't. If they had turned around and taken a look at the other side of the building, they would have seen the main entrance. Employees were inside, but they didn't see them either. The man and his daughter left without getting any results. Not really trying to find out why it seemed to them the place was locked. Now, think about it, the time they spent was completely wasted. You go and you make an effort but without getting any results. If someone asked you would say "I went, I tried." Yes, you went, and you tried, but where is the result? We should get results after our efforts.

I have a friend who came to me one day and said: "Yesterday I thought about getting some dessert for you and bringing it with me today". Then, he listed so many excuses for not bringing it. So, did we get to eat the dessert? No. This is a simple example, but our daily lives are filled with these kinds of situations. We do not try hard enough to get results. No need to tell me about your intentions if there were no results. We would have excuses like, "I went, I wandered around, I was there, I went back..." Ok, but did you get the result? If we don't get results after our plans, then it is better to not even speak about it.

GOVERNANCE

The most important management skill is to be able to manage your own nature, which is the bigger universe. Instead, we are grappling with minor issues. We are the governor of the bigger universe; of ourselves. Anything below that is not worthy of us.

This is why we are going into distress. When you can govern yourself, you will be able to easily govern daily tasks as well. If we govern one, we can govern the other.

I notice that many managers are not aware enough of what is happening around them, like if their office doors are locked at night or what's in those piles on their desks. Days come and go like this. We only check certain things out of habit. This is not what management is. Let me tell you about what the common outlook of management in general is. If the bills and loans are paid and there is still some money left, you are happy. This is not management. Firstly, I will manage my own nature. After that, I will manage my dealings with the ones who are closest to me. For me, the closest is my family. After that, my work. You see, firstly myself: my character and personality. Then my family, work and profession. After that, my social life.

WE MUST HAVE ENOUGH KNOWLEDGE FOR OURSELVES

As a business owner do you call your accountant from time to time to check in on the finances or is your accountant running it all? You will have no issues in accounting if you are in control. Many traders lose in accounting. That means that we need to have enough information about any field we get ourselves into. In other words; I will not necessarily become an accountant or a foreman, but I will get enough knowledge about the different goings-on in my business. But many business owners are putting the burden on people who work for them. You see, the real reason they put the responsibility on others is that they don't have enough knowledge to supervise. If something happens, they will say, "I trusted them". It's not really about trust, but lack of knowledge. As a result, the business owner is in a vulnerable position. At some point they will have to face problems and they surely will. These problems could be about the promises they make, or about the treatment of people, or it could be about the quality, the money they make or some other thing, for sure.

Deception

Firstly, we should deal with dishonest people without taking a dishonest stance ourselves. We should be mindful of how we approach others. Look, if you call a young man a tiger, they will take that as a compliment. But if you call someone a snake, that's an insult. If you say someone is like a bee, working hard, they will be proud. But if you call them a chicken, it could cause a fight. If you call someone a lion that would be flattering. But if you said rat, they would be pissed. These are all names of animals, but they have very different connotations. It's very important how we approach people. Everyone has their own ordeal. Everyone needs some encouraging words and a smile.

Secondly, do not try to cheat the cheater, just dodge them instead. If you try to cheat the cheater, you stoop to their level. You can say things like, "I am not available", "I do not have what you need", or something along the lines. Do I ever get deceived? Yes, it happens to me too. It is not really possible to avoid it completely. But the thing is; we should get through it with the least amount of harm. We, at least, need to have the same level of protection as a bank. For example, a bank is deceived by one out of a hundred customers. But tradesmen, let's say, are deceived by twenty percent. This means that we must get through every case with the least amount of damage.

No one can make me co-sign a loan. No one would even think about asking. Not even my nearest and dearest can get me to sign. Why? Because I become responsible when I sign that. I wouldn't vouch for just anyone. Even if you say that you have a lot of property for collateral, that doesn't really matter. Once you co-sign the loan, the damage is done. There are also people who come to me saying: "We came to you because you are who we feel close to." Not really. They most likely went out, paid a visit to everyone they know, and I was the last one left. One day, a loved one came to visit me and said, "I could have gone to someone else but I wanted to come here". I said "Come on, you have searched and searched and when you could not find a better alternative... "Well, to be honest, that's true", he admitted. So, these are things that we can easily fall for.

INCREASING EFFICIENCY

Big supermarkets or stores should write down the inquiries they get. They should keep a list. If something is requested once or twice a day, it should be purchased and added to the stock. The local shopkeeper in a small rural town knows this, but here in the big city, the more sophisticated business owners may not. There are some things that come with being educated in the school of life. They should observe. Their brains should always work around what customers are doing, where they are stopping, where they are leaning. It should be a competition, and a bonus should be given to those with success. The employees would not stay idle if there is a bonus or say 20% of profit is given to those who are efficient in the workplace. "I do my job better than most, this is enough for me", you may say. See, this "enough" word kills a person. You must constantly research the market and develop. Do you know how many factories there are in the country you are operating in that produce the same goods? Or how many in the world?

Or what kind of innovations are out there? Why don't we research this in our spare time? Why do we sit idly and waste our valuable time?

BENEFITING OR HARMING PEOPLE

Let's say you are a car manufacturer. What is your priority? Your priority is profit. Do you do any research about the substances in the material which you use for cars, to see if they are harmful to people or not? No, you don't. See, this is not a humane approach. Some of those materials are harmful to humans. But producers ignore that. They say that the radiation emitted by cell phones is harming people, so why are they still doing it? Would a decent person do this? This is what I am trying to say. It is not my intention to slander anyone.

We are using fertilizers to increase our wheat crop. Why don't we make the same effort to improve the taste or flavor? Because our profit grows when our crop increases, then why does the taste matter? This is the tricky part. Do I place greater value on humanity or profit? This should not be hard to answer. Not hard, if we had some morals and virtues. If we would have some morals and virtues like fifty or sixty years ago, when we could leave our doors unlocked.

When producing fabric, how much time do they spend thinking if that fabric is useful or harmful to people? Why are they producing it if it is harmful to me? Why are they making us wear harmful materials? Why are they selling us bad products and presenting them as good? For profit. A person with a focus on profit cannot master a profession. In this context, there is no honesty nor integrity. Instead, exploitation begins, and where exploitation begins humanity ends.

A person should take pride in their profession. Our brains should work 24 hours a day about what's useful for humans. Whatever we produce should be beneficial to people. But today what we're seeing is mostly exploitation. Business practices are mostly about exploiting the customers. They are always thinking about how to cheapen the product.

Making money is different than being successful. The moment I start to think about making money, I become an exploiter. That means the moment I think about making money, my conscience does not work anymore. But the moment I become successful; the money will come naturally. Success comes with earning people's trust and respect.

A TRUE HUMAN ENHANCES

All things on earth are here for our use. But if we allow them to control us, we are in violation of our own nature. We are supposed to justly regulate the material world that is meant to serve us. But when you are on the side of exploitation, you might, for example, artificialize vegetables and grains in the name of increasing their quantity. If you were a true human, you would instead think about how to improve the taste and offer it to people. A true human would not make all those fruits and tomatoes so artificial. They would offer produce that is sweeter, tastier, healthier, and of good quality, and wouldn't just sell it for the sake of making a profit. The current commercial mentality is rotten to the core. They cheapen and cheapen their offerings and then sell it to people. And they call this innovation. Why can't innovation work the other way around as well? Humans have the ability to make produce bigger and in greater quantities, we have that authority. So why don't we also add some more flavor, some more taste. If you innovated on quantity, you could innovate on quality also. But no, you say to yourself, "I would rather earn quick money."

In the economy, we should put humans first. If what we are wearing is harmful to people, it shouldn't be produced. Harmful food should not be produced. Being moral should be the priority, as honor and human dignity come first. If you are a true human, it's most important to make your products better and more beneficial to humans. There should be idea-generating circles in companies where the goal is to find what things in nature can be found and turned into a product for the benefit of people.

WORK ETHIC

Let me tell you how most people work. Even the best ones go to the workplace and stay there for eight hours, but their minds are not there. They take their bodies to the workplace, but their minds are elsewhere. They think about their cars, bills, spouses, children... Right at the end of the work day, they pack up and say, "Let's go". Can we say the salary that people make this way is truly deserved when employers are paying workers for their minds? A worker's job is to invent and innovate there. If your job is to produce a cup, you should spend day and night finding a way to make that cup more efficient, and after that, become a partner to your boss one day. This is how the economy should work.

As a manufacturer how do we do business honestly? It's easy. Let's say we are manufacturing textiles. For example, if fifty threads per fabric are supposed to be added, weavers usually make it forty-five or forty-six. Though we could add fifty-one. Do the other manufacturers produce with thirty percent cotton? We could do with thirty-one percent. If the payment day is usually on the twentieth, we can make it on the fifteenth. You also have an advantage if you don't need to take out a loan from a bank. The ones who take out loans will need to add the interest they pay, on top of the price. So, we can charge less but make more profit than others. When the customer checks the quality of the fabric, they will see that there are fifty-one threads and thirty-one percent cotton. This way you earn their trust and start a long-lasting business relationship. Besides, you would proudly present your product to anyone and even encourage them to question the quality. However, how would the ones who weave with forty-six threads instead of fifty explain themselves? Is cheapening the product really worth the embarrassment?

BEING FAIR

We are all exploiting nature and we never give anything back. Recently I asked a big leather producer: "The ones who enable you to build a fortune are the shepherds looking after the herds. Do you ever go and visit them?" Just take a look at what you are wearing; so many of those materials are the works of shepherds. What are your belts, your shoes, your jackets made of? Leather and textile manufacturers are dependent on the shepherds, and yet they never thank them. There is nobody saying: "Thank you for your service, we all gained our wealth because of you". As I always talk about this, I heard that just recently a manufacturer did pay a visit. They went together with the manager. The shepherd was surprised when they said: "Send your children to our factory, we will show them the production. We got rich thanks to your work." We have become so short-sighted that we can't even think about the things that make our business what it is. The factory owner's children should go visit the shepherd and the shepherd's children should go visit the factory, so that there is fairness.

CHAPTER 2

ECONOMY

What is the economy? The economy is the use of nature for the benefit of people. It is the transformation of nature for the welfare of people. For example, we make cement from rock, we use water to make electricity, we produce clothes from cotton. The economy is the equitable distribution of this transformation. It unites people and nature in a fair, lawful, and pleasant way.

What is the economy good for? There are five main aspects of the economy. Eating-drinking, clothing, protection (defense), mobility (transportation), and resting (hospitals, music, relaxation). The economy is comprised of these five areas, and no other.

There is no real economy in the world right now, there is only exploitation. One type of modern economy is "intelligence-capital". The other type is "labor-capital". Both intelligence-capital and labor-capital are the games of profiteers and exploiters. One is based on labor, it uses people like machines; the other one is based on shrewdness, exploiting with intelligence. What else is there?

From the perspective of a true human, we should have "Labor-Intelligence". Labor and intelligence should go hand in hand. We cannot have only intelligence without labor. Because it is against our true nature. Otherwise, exploitation begins. Mind you, there are textile products woven by machines that are very cheap. When it's knit by a person, the same product's price would be much higher. Why is that? Because a lot of labor and intelligence is added. We have to have both labor and intelligence.

So, what is the current economy established on? On capital, on exploitation. For one thing, right from the beginning, it is a deception, because there can be no honesty where there is capital. Because money, which is just a piece of paper, is earning on its own. When we say capital, we are talking about the earnings obtained without expending labor and intelligence. Capital generates interest. Because of the income that we receive without effort, earning interest devastates us.

The extravagance, the luxury, the fashion that are by-products of interest, devastate us. From the perspective of the true human; the meaning of interest is, making an income for free, without earning it. Anything we obtain without labor and intelligence is an interest. If you get some knowledge from someone and then tell other people about it as if you are the source of that knowledge, that is also an interest. Do not think of the term interest with a narrow meaning.

THE SYSTEM WAS ESTABLISHED BY EXPLOITERS

Some people are saying the economic system is going to collapse. It sure would. The way the current system is built is bound to create poverty. It is not for the good of people. When poverty spreads, the gap is widened and there can be even further exploitation. At one point, ideologues rose up claiming to defend the rights of workers. Everyone thought it was an attempt to defend the rights of workers against factory owners. In that case, what are lockouts and strikes? If there is animosity between workers and owners, can we talk about the quality of production there? We couldn't even see that. Can there be any success at home if you always fight with those in your house? So, what have they done? They have turned employees against their owners, which actually ends up benefiting owners more than workers. When there is a strike, that would be the owners' excuse to increase prices and sell the goods in their inventory for a higher amount. So, the whole system has been serving exploitation. Mixed economies, left-wings, right-wings, they have all served the same purpose and eventually, it all came to the brink of bankruptcy.

MOVING FROM THE BROKEN ECONOMIC SYSTEM

The current economic system is in a quagmire all around the world. We can't point to a place where it isn't. The ones that we praise are just better off than the rest. Name a state in the modern economy that is not in a mess, not to mention in moral and ethical collapse.

Once we decide to move to an economy that is in line with true human nature, we may have some problems in the initial transition period. We also may have capital in the transition. But the goal would be an economy without capital, based on labor and intelligence. It is an economic system in which people live in their natural state. There is nothing but labor and intelligence. Intelligence alone is exploitation. Labor alone is another kind of exploitation. These two should go together.

EMPLOYEE - EMPLOYER

In this economic system, in the factories, there should be a maximum of three people with ownership responsibility. They should receive a salary for the responsibility they carry. This is the pay given for using their intelligence due to taking on the responsibility. If they physically work in the factory, they should receive an additional salary for working. So, there can't be a boss like we have today, who would earn a profit just because of the capital they invest in. The thing is, in current systems, the foundations are broken and the boss and the employees are at odds. The system was built on the conflict between those two. Be fair, what good can come when the boss and the employees are at odds? Can there be any success, or humanity, where the employer does not see his employee as his son, and an employee does not see his employer as his father, and doesn't feel that warmth at work?

From the true-human perspective, everyone should be productive in the economy. Everyone's labor and intelligence should be appropriately rewarded. The owners would not sit idly at the company and make money with no effort. They would get paid in return for their responsibility, and if they work, they get a salary for that as well. Otherwise, how could we find balance? How could we be fair and just?

Taxation

Taxation in the economy should be done only in one way. Here is how it should work: Fifty percent of earnings would go to the government. The government would dedicate half of that to salaries and expenses. The other half would be saved for the future. Regarding the remaining fifty percent that goes to the individuals, half would be used for our living expenses and half would be saved for our future. This is how the economy should be. There is no interest, there is no deceit, there is service, there is production; there is no waste but frugality instead. How are we going to spend this abundance? The shoes, the clothes we wear will only cost a fraction of what we pay now. Today; middlemen and interest are destroying us. They all add to the cost of goods. If there were no middlemen in economies, twenty-five percent of what we earn would be enough for our livelihood.

CAPITAL

The economy is the affair of labor and intelligence, not of capital. Capital is money earned without putting in labor and intelligence. Capital feeds off the producers without expending labor and intelligence. It is money earned without producing. It doesn't involve physical labor, only intelligence. However, what people earn with their own labor and intelligence and invest in their own businesses, is not capital; it is a contribution to production.

We do not have a problem with the banks themselves. Let this not be misunderstood. We have a problem with the system. A piece of paper –money-, comes in between labor and intelligence, dominating them. This piece of paper earns more than you do. We can't have this. This piece of paper has no hands, no feet, no tongue. So how is that it earns?

There is no place for humanity when capital enters

Wherever we have capital; honesty, dignity, and modesty are eroded. Capital destroys them. No one can argue otherwise. Slavery and chaos all exist where there is capital. In places where capital rules, there is no more the notion of being a true human. Because wherever there is capital, there are also middlemen, and middlemen live off others. Wherever there is capital, there is interest and making money with no labor. Wherever there is capital, there is squandering. There is extravagance and opulence. There is exploitation. Capital enters little by little and leaves no honor, dignity, or modesty. Why? Because everything other than labor and intelligence diminishes the dignity of a person. People are honored for their labor and intelligence. How can a piece of paper with no hands and feet, earn as much as a living being? When this is removed, the competition of labor and intelligence begins, and success emerges.

Where there is capital, there comes greed for money. There is no intention of bettering the life quality and improving the integrity of humans but rather, marketing unhealthy foods and synthetic fabrics without considering if all those things are good for people or not. Why? Because the priority is not given to humans. The priority is given to exploiting and making money off of humans.

Wherever there is capital, there are also middlemen, brokers, and financiers. When middlemen are involved and interest is added on top of the price, it will cost us multiple times its true value. In many products, the bulk of the profit is going to the middlemen instead of producers. What we are saying is, that prices should only reflect the value of the labor and intelligence put in. When only the value of labor and intelligence was used in the past, one parent's income was enough to raise nine, or ten children. Today everyone in the family is working, and yet, there is not enough income for everyday living expenses.

THE MIDDLEMEN

We need to get rid of the middlemen. This will help us gain our integrity. The middlemen are exploiting us. We have become captive. We are bound to the local middleman, that middleman is bound to the one above him, that one to the one above him, and it goes up this way. That is how it works. Consider the retail system of a tire dealership. A new retailer opens in a small town. He buys a new home. The retailer then expands to the big city, and he buys a building. After that, he expands throughout the region and buys a yacht. Finally, he expands nationwide and buys a private jet. This is how the middlemen are supported. All the money of poor laborers goes to the middlemen. Then we get into financial difficulties because the price of a tire goes up multiple times. For a whole year, a farmer is dealing with the fertilizers, maintenance, watering, hoeing, while the middlemen reap millions just by sitting around. This needs to end. When we dismiss the middlemen and interest, the product that sells for a hundred will be sold for only a fraction of that, and the buyers will keep their money in their pockets.

WHO IS RESPONSIBLE FOR THIS OVERPRICING?

If you are not the manufacturer of what you are selling, you are a middleman. There is another one above you, and another one above him. All are using credit from the banks and adding the interest rate on top of their profit margin. What happens is; the prices get jacked up. If the manufacturer is using a loan, aren't they going to add the interest they pay on top of the price? Then when the goods come to the wholesaler, aren't they going to add the loan's interest to their price? Isn't the retailer also going to add it? As a result of all this, prices become significantly higher than what they would have been without the interest. So, what's causing all this increase in prices? The middleman's margins and the interest. When we have middlemen in between, then we will have interest, trickery, deceit, and hoarding, and so on.

There will be no middlemen in our system. Every producer labels their product with the price printed on its packaging, and it will be sold at that price everywhere within the country. Anything that goes on sale will carry the brand of the producer and they will be responsible for what they produce. The ones responsible for selling will make only a small profit, that's worth as much as the labor and intelligence they put into the process. Let's say we have a product that has a price of 10. How much is the cost of the labor and intelligence of the seller? Let's say it's 1; that will be printed on the goods and sold for 11. It is that simple. Labor and intelligence will lead. There will be no middlemen.

MONEY

Years ago, there was no talk of money. Seriously, no one used to talk about money. Such a person would be left alienated from society at that time. Let me give you an example. One of our friends owned a dealership. He sold a motorcycle and, on that day, he received some money. Silk white shirts were in fashion at that time. He put the money in his front pocket, joined us, and sat down. We all looked at his pocket as the money was clearly visible. We reprimanded him for being showy. It was a disgrace to do that in those days, a big disgrace. After that embarrassment, our friend left town, moved to the capital, and still hasn't come back. It's not good manners to be talking about money. What has happened to us, we keep talking about it these days? We have fallen for the traps of exploiters and money has become all that people think about. Having money is one thing, but holding money above your character is another.

MONEY IS A VALUE MEASUREMENT

What is money? It is a value measurement corresponding to our labor and intelligence. In the past, the villagers brought grapes to the city and bought wheat. There was no money, they would exchange it. You brought beans, I brought chickpeas, and goods were exchanged. There was only an exchange of goods. The money came much later. It came together with problems.

Money is only a value measurement. Not everyone is aware of this. If money is a value measurement, like meter or kilogram, and if everywhere in the world the meter is a hundred centimeters, if everywhere the kilogram is a thousand grams, why is money measured differently for the wealthy and the poor countries? In today's world, the currency of the wealthy nations is valuable, and the currency of the poor ones is worthless. The wealthy can change the value of money as they wish. How is that fair? The value of money should be the same everywhere. One Lira should be the same Lira everywhere in the world. Though, it all comes down to power. The powerful call the shots in every era.

EARNING MONEY AND SUCCESS

We shouldn't do our job just for a living, for economic reasons, or to earn money. Rather, we should aim for success. If your only aim is to make money, that would lead to exploitation. There is no place for humanity where this happens. But if I am successful and if I provide my service to people, the money will come naturally.

Where there is life, success is never ending. Success is a result of productivity. It must be provided to people. For example, if you are a very good barber and you offer services to people, this is a success. What I mean is that something cannot be a success if it is not provided to people. And you see, when your idea is provided to the whole world, such as the use of electricity, this will be a great success.

The standard is to do what's worthy of being a human. This standard is what the competition should be about, instead of focusing on making money. These are two different things; earning money, and being successful. The two of them seem the same, but actually, they are polar opposites. One is exploitation, and the other is humanity. This is because when you are successful; trust is not broken, respect is not lost, and you keep your character. But if your only goal is to make money, you would earn by compromising quality while deceiving and cheating. You will not do these things if you give priority to your success, profession, and your good name. When you are the best at what you do, you do not need to worry about money anyway. It comes naturally.

LIFE IS ABOUT TRUST

When somebody mentions trading, money comes to mind. If money comes to mind there is no such thing as trade anymore. When you think of trade; production, trust, and respect should come to your mind. Can there be trade if there is no trust? The economic system that we propose is built on respect and trust. Our lives should be all about trust. Betrayal of trust is actually a crime.

The one whose goal is to make money does not know anything. He has a small mind and only knows a few methods to make money. And those kinds of people who you envy are actually cowardly and pathetic. There are no other people who worry about their livelihood as much as they do. I always speak from facts. How so? Because I have been there. After I removed those ideas from my life, only then did I become free. I realized then; that those are the things I do not need at all. Those are trivial things not deemed to be important. In reality, there were other things that I needed. I need my character, my honor, and my dignity. I should not put myself in a position where I can't look someone in the eye.

WEALTH

In order for someone to be called wealthy, they need to be a producer and also produce more than they consume. Produce whatever you can. Produce sugar, flowers, ethics, honor, good clothing, speeches, good manners, a restaurant, food, or do whatever you can. We should become producers. And we should produce more than we consume. And we should redistribute that extra supply. That is what makes a person wealthy; not those who merely accumulate. They simply add a building to buildings, a machine to machines, an estate to estates. What they are really doing is slavery on their part.

In the process of accumulating wealth, the rich are servants first and then slaves after they have their wealth. This is not the meaning of being rich. Accumulating goods is not wealth. It is poverty. This includes all the people you call rich. Let me explain what I mean. All those neglected summer houses and mansions; aren't their owners now a slave to those properties? They need to pay taxes on them, they need to do this and that. Isn't this slavery? Wherever I go, I find a nice hotel and I stay there. For example, there is a beautiful hotel in this tourist destination that I went to. I wanted to meet with the owner, and in the morning, he joined me for breakfast. I saw that he does not do anything but work. He gave me the upper corner room, and I was very comfortable, I thanked him for that. I asked him: "Tell me the truth, have you ever stayed in any of these rooms and gotten that comfortable?". He said: "Never". This is what you call rich; someone carrying around all these assets on their back.

CREATING AND DISTRIBUTING WEALTH

Our goals cannot be material objects because they are already at our disposal. Materials do not talk, they do not say anything; all these materials, paper, stone, flowers, they do not speak. It's normal to have these things, that is just the way things should be. But humans are not supposed to only accumulate goods, we are supposed to spend what we earn on humanity. We got used to accumulating. A person who owns a factory works toward owning another one, in addition to what he already has. Our motivation is wrong. It is misunderstood. To be rich is to produce and then distribute. This can be done in ethics, humanity, service, you name it.

You have to look at what we said from all perspectives, not only from one. So, when somebody talks about being poor, you would immediately think about money. This is not the right way to look at it. You are the greatest creation of God, and if you do not utilize this greatness then you are poor. There is no greater being than you on the Earth. Comprehend and apply this. If you don't, you are poor. Think very generally. Are we poor emotionally? Are we poor physically? Are we poor sensually? Are we poor in our guidance?

YOU ARE WEALTHY BY NATURE

Someone can be wealthy, or can be middle class, but never poor. When you shake that poor person up and get them to change their mindset, a new way of thinking would emerge and old conditioning would be broken. A person falls into poverty because of a few habits. For example, are you determined? Do you have enough knowledge about your profession? Are you brave? If so, you are wealthy. That's it. It is that simple. Once you get rid of poverty, you become wealthy.

Poverty is one thing that nature, God, the Universe dislikes the most. Do you know why? Because you are wealthy by nature. How can people be poor, when they were given so much wisdom to use?

We always say; that in order for you to become alive, you should never use these words: "Not possible" and "I can't". When it comes to economic resurgence, I would use the words: "Possible" and "I can". Moreover, there are three main pillars of the economy. Be determined, be brave, and be informed. Anyone who meets these would be rich. By nature, everyone has the potential to be wealthy anyway. I'm talking about all this from the true-human perspective. Do not mistake these concepts for things that are fleeting.

Some of you want a factory. But a human being is already a huge factory. Material possessions should not be the ultimate goal. Such ambitions would be shameful for an industrious, organized, neat, principled, hardworking, honest, serious, intelligent person.

FIVE IDOLS

You have five idols that you envy: wealth, lust, fame, influence, and status. People who have these in their lives also have a lot of problems. You cannot find anyone with these idols who can say they are happy.

How can it be that I will be happy by oppressing others, getting mad at others, and exploiting others? This is just not compatible with our nature.

I went to visit a friend who has an office across from this giant corporation. I said to him you have become a neighbor to this corporate giant. He smiled sheepishly. I said, why are you doubting yourself? Then I asked, "Do you have any issues with your bank?" No, he answered. "Have you taken out any loans?" No, he said. "Do you have any obligations with the local authorities?" No, he answered again. How about with politicians?" No. Then I said, the owner of that corporation is oppressed by these very things day and night. He has to spend all his time buttering up these politicians and authorities just to achieve his own aims. Why do you not consider yourself superior? It was then that he came to his senses. From morning to evening, you'd have to keep asking if there are any orders, chasing the administration on any new requests. This is the life of the wealthy.

One day, a very wealthy friend of mine invited me to come over for a cup of tea. By coincidence, some bank manager was also visiting him. I was disturbed by how timidly my friend behaved around the bank manager. I'd rather have less money, or say eighty million as opposed to a hundred, than have no authority, and have to suck up to the banker. We can't even imagine thinking this way. If I would end up sitting timidly opposite that banker, what good is all that wealth I have? We do not realize that if I am oppressed in one situation, I will eventually oppress someone else in another. That is because there is the law of give and take in life. If you are being oppressed, you will also oppress.

SHOPPING

When one only does business with the one place that they are used to, they get deceived. When we are shopping, we should visit at least five different places. We should ask questions and gather information. When we do the research, we learn about different product qualities and types. We would understand whether that seller is doing us a favor, or if they are trying to deceive us. The issue is, when we research, we learn for our own benefit. I am frustrated with those who always buy goods from the same place. They would have no knowledge, there is no room for improvement because they buy from the same place; the place that they are used to. I always do the opposite.

I used to have a view that considered bargaining as shameful. Then later, this one time I went to a distant town far away from where I lived. Forty, fifty years ago, that town used to have cheap prices. I would go there for bargaining and shopping. There was one instance I never could forget; I bought something for 30 instead of 100. At first, the seller went down to 70. I went there twice offering 30. He told me to leave. He said angrily "Don't you understand, that's my final price.", before eventually giving in to my low offer. I'll always remember that. But I don't remember the other shopping I did. Why? Because they were just ordinary exchanges. Buy it if you like it, don't if you don't. That incident in that distant town was when I overcame the barrier in my head that bargaining was shameful. If I hadn't had that experience, I wouldn't have been able to bargain in my hometown among people I knew. That would have been shameful. But if you don't bargain, you will get ripped off.

NOT KNOWING THE PROFESSION OF SHOPPING

You are always misled when you do not know how to properly shop. The shopping you know is only one method. It is out of habit. When you hear about successful shopping, you mostly think of buying at a cheap price. But in shopping, we should be learning about different product qualities, different types and we should learn about the market. Why would I go shopping only to merely complete a transaction? Say I went out to buy water, I bought it and came back home. That's not in your best interest. I would check how many different types of water there are, what are the differences between them, why one is more expensive than the other etc. Once your mind opens up to this idea about shopping, it will open up to other ideas as well.

This one time, I went to buy some clothes with my mentor. My mentor whispered something in the seller's ear. Outside I asked him what happened. "I asked him for a fifty percent discount", he said. Then I asked him why he whispered his request. He replied, "There was another customer around, would he have given me a discount if they also heard it?" And then he continued, "If the seller agrees with your offer, he would say 'just wait here, I'll deal with this other customer' ". So, the moral of the story is that, if there are other customers present, you should make sure only the seller hears your offer.

The Issue is to Buy for its True Value

The issue is not necessarily the money, but to pay the good's true value. For example, one florist offers a flower for 500, but another one offers it for 100. That is a big difference, isn't it? You go and buy the cheaper one. But then that cheaper one looks awful the whole year and you regret the purchase. If you had taken the more expensive one, you would have been impressed by how beautiful it would have looked. And even though you see this difference, the second time again you may find the cheaper one more appealing. But you got fooled once and that flower is your joy. You pay more money, but it's worth it because it is something that you will be looking at every day. We are not aware of this notion; we don't know enough about the principles of shopping. What we buy should be of good quality, it should be practical. For example, every day, I sit in my office chair for at least four hours. The office chair is very valuable to me. I need to get the best. This has nothing to do with money. We have so many habitual mindsets that harm us, which we are not fully aware of.

WASTEFULNESS - FRUGALITY

The economy's greatest enemy is wastefulness. Its greatest friend is frugality. Let us reflect on ourselves, how much do we waste? Did you know that the biggest waste of all is the misuse of time? On the contrary, you just want the time to pass by somehow. Anything that is inefficient is a waste.

There should be no wastefulness, you should eliminate the wastefulness in your life and you should be frugal. You should conserve what you have. What is conserving? Firstly, you should conserve your own things, starting with your mind. For example, I never go anywhere just to do one thing. With one effort, a lot of different things can be taken care of. I wouldn't go all the way downtown just to do one thing. Even if I go to a restaurant, I take care of various tasks along the way. I can complete several things at one time. Taking care of only one thing when you go out is unproductive.

THE ONE WHO WASTES BECOMES NEEDY

There is no law and order where there is waste. Are you aware of how much waste there is in workplaces and factories? A person who is wasteful eventually becomes needy. A wasteful person is immoral. A frugal person has integrity. That quality is achieved by practicing it, awareness is not enough. Their every frugal behavior benefits other people, though it may be indirectly. To be frugal is to give everything its true value. It doesn't mean being stingy.

One pillar of the economy is being frugal. Those who are not, end up going broke. You will also go broke if you leave your work unfinished. Those are two legs we will stand on. We should finish what we start. This is what a promise means. This is trust. And if we are also frugal, then we will stand on our own two feet.

Expense – Waste

I like expenditure. Expenditure is one thing, squandering is another. Expenditure is needed. Squandering is wasting what is needed. For example, a cleaning cloth that we wipe the glass with can be made out of old rags in the house. But people immediately throw these kinds of things away. Sometimes I see garbage bins where I live; if I weren't ashamed, I would go down and get those plastic bags and plastic bottles. What's interesting is, that this act of conservation is always done by impoverished people. Not making use of what's in the garbage is a waste. To pour polluted water into a river is a waste. To ruin such beautiful places is a waste.

My way of being frugal while shopping is, that I have never purchased expensive clothes. All my clothes are fifteen, twenty years old. I always use local products, maybe with the exception of a special gift. This is what I believe. I try my best. We as individuals form a whole. If everyone would think this way, we would have no problems left.

GIVING PRIORITY TO PEOPLE

I prioritize the human character and integrity, and I serve people and I benefit in return. The reward for my work comes naturally. This is one thing, and prioritizing money is another. This is a common thing in today's society; to prioritize money. When I talk about this, some business owners say: "But I am providing for hundreds of people". Ok, but are you doing it for nothing in return? You make money off of their labor. Does the business owner think about their employees as much as his children? No. See, then there is no humanity there.

We get paid for our hard work and intelligence. But the priority should be service to the people. How can I leave my humanity aside and go after material goals that will end up in the garbage or in the toilet? Those who prioritize money will spend it on what? On the things that eventually go into the garbage or into the toilet. Because if the way you earn money is not befitting human integrity, then that kind of income is bound to go to waste and extravagance.

VALUING PEOPLE

Serving people means success. Now, think of a grocery store. Customers come in every day. It is one thing to value that person as a human being; it is another just to see them as a potential purchaser. When you say, 'a person has come in', instead of a "customer", you give priority to people.

We should do everything in business according to the honor and dignity of humans. The current system is designed with money as the priority. There is no humanity in this system. When the system is designed based on the honor and integrity of the human, money will come naturally as a reward for the labor and intelligence put in. The basis is important, the priority is important. Is the priority the human's honor and integrity or is it our stomach? One's dignity, pride, and honor should be considered most important. For example, whichever setting we're in, we're responsible for each other's clarity of mind. The slightest negative word may disturb the other person's mind. A simple positive word may clarify their mind. You look at someone the wrong way for a moment, and they wonder: "Why did he look at me like that?", which might cause distress for days. But if you give a beautiful smile, they will be happy. Why are we not sharing more positiveness with people? Why do we see them with negativity? What would we lose if we smiled, if we looked at them with positivity, if we uttered some positive words? Is there someone stopping us from doing all this? These are very simple but very important things. Why would we hide those gifts from people when God has given them to serve humans?

"

All the goodness, successes and good virtues there are in the world, exist within every human's core.